The Raw Meat Cat Food Cookbook

Published by Velluminous Press
www.velluminous.com

Copyright ©2013 Holly Ollivander & Huw Thomas

ISBN: 978-1-905605-39-2

cover illustration by Holly Ollivander

this book is dedicated
to the beloved memory of
SPIKE OREO THOMAS

Spikey, we wish we'd known then
what we know now.

Contents

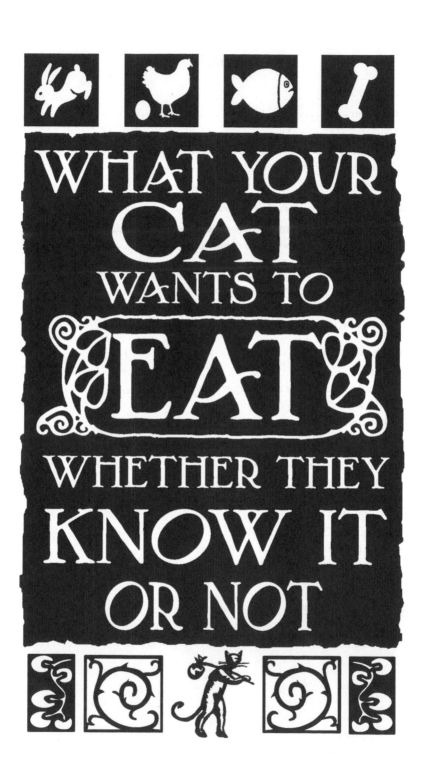

WHAT YOUR CAT WANTS TO EAT WHETHER THEY KNOW IT OR NOT

Introduction

Chances are, you have picked up this book because you share your life with one or more of the marvelous, complex and emotionally rewarding entities that are cats. You wish them to experience a long and happy life with you, and you are willing to go to some effort to give them that.

If that's the case, welcome to the *Raw Meat Cat Food Cookbook*!

Where We're Coming From

In 2004, our beloved 18-month-old cat Mehetabel lost control of her bladder on our white duvet cover. It was only a small amount of urine but what we found alarming was that it was tinged pink. Over the next few years we would learn more about feline urinary-tract health but at the time the following terrifying equation was what came to mind:

$$urine + blood = imminent\ kidney\ failure + death\ of\ our\ cat$$

We rushed Mehetabel to the vet, who prescribed antibiotics and a urine test and who—to our relief—seemed fairly unconcerned. The antibiotics appeared to clear up the problem in short order. However, when the urine test results came back, it turned out Mehetabel was suffering from struvite crystals which form when a cat's urine is not acid enough.

Left untreated, these crystals can cut, scar, cause swelling, and eventually block the cat's urethra permanently. The vet recommended switching Mehetabel away from her then-current food (a premium brand of dry kibble) to a medicated brand formulated to acidify urine. We went away with the new food, hoping that all would now be well.

And so it was, kind of...

Mehetabel still suffered a relapse every few months, but by keeping her on the medicated food, plus administering water from a silicone bulb, plus getting antibiotics whenever a blockage/infection flared up... it wasn't ideal but it seemed to be the best we could hope for. We soldiered on with Mehetabel's health issues, using the "official" ways of dealing with them, for the next six years or so.

However, in 2010, another of our cats began to display similar symptoms. Jet was about 11 years old at the time (she came to us as a young adult stray), and had been losing weight and condition despite adoring her commercial, individual (wet) packet food. She was passing what we could only assume were crystals; her bright red urine contained small, glistening, mucus-balls that could easily have been mistaken for parts of her insides. We got the test results we expected and put her on the recommended acidifying diet, but she kept going downhill and continued to pass blood and mucus.

It was time to acknowledge that the vet, armed mainly with a selection of drugs and commercial diets, could not provide a long-term remedy. That's not to belittle the veterinarian profession in any way; it's just that if a problem requires a re-think by an animal's *owner*, then the animal's *vet* is clearly not the person who needs to provide a solution.

After extensive research into commercial cat food it became clear that the diet we had chosen (with the best intentions) to feed our cats, was the root of the problem. At best, the medicated cat food contained additives that attempted to compensate for some of the harm that the other ingredients were causing. The solution was obvious and we took it: we switched to the raw food diet we describe in this book.

Jet in particular has always been a fussy eater and took a little persuading, but we persisted and succeeded in getting both cats to accept the new diet. Two years later, all our cats are using their litter trays and passing normal urine, free of blood or stones. None are dependent upon medication or antibiotics.

Our most recent arrival, Penny, came to us as a five week-old kitten having been rejected by her mother and subsequently hand-reared by one of our local vets, then briefly weaned onto commercial food. We immediately offered her raw meat food and she fell on it as if it was something she'd been missing as much as she surely missed her mother's milk. Penny has been exclusively fed (apart from the very occasional human-mealtime indulgence) on raw meat food for the entire time she's been with us now, and is a thriving and growing six-month-old.

What's more, having discovered raw food she turned up her nose at the commercial food we'd been given by the vet "just in case". She wanted the real thing.

Can we guarantee that this raw meat diet will have the same miraculous effects on your cat, as it did on ours? Of course we can't. All we can do is share the techniques and recipes that have worked for us in the sincere hope that they will work for you as well.

The Problem with Grain-based Commercial Cat Food

The tagline to this book says, *"What your cat wants to eat, whether they know it or not,"* because most modern cats simply do not know what they have been missing. Since the moment they were weaned, they have become addicted to a corporate-formulated substance that can eventually destroy every major organ of the feline body: grain-dominant cat food. This addiction can adversely affect blood sugar, urine pH, adrenal stability, digestive function, and tooth, gum and joint health, and our experience is that it can be a major contributor to spiraling vet bills after the age of four or five years old.

For six-plus decades, commercial grain-based cat food has been pushed upon the public for one main reason: corporate profit. Regrettably, it isn't just cats who are addicted; advertising has brainwashed humans into believing that feeding our obligate carnivore companions a meat-flavored, grain-based diet is the best way to show how much we care.

Another potential source of pressure is the funding of certain veterinary colleges by major pet food manufacturers. They assure any doubters that such funding is ethical and even-handed … which would mean that the corporations are acting in the best interests of their consumers (who are of course our pets!) rather than seeking to create recommendations and outlets for the corporation's products without ever addressing the issue of whether *any* brand can be good within a whole class of products that are harmful.

This concern can only be heightened when you consider how many manufacturers offer specially-tailored supplemental cat foods to deal with the health problems their products originally exacerbated.

Cats are obligate carnivores; they require muscle meat, bones and organs, rather than grain, in order to operate at peak health. If pet food companies offered for sale what a cat really needs, once the more complicated production costs were met and then a percentage of profit added on top to keep the shareholders happy, the cat-owning public would simply balk at paying that much. Grain is a cheap filler, meat is not, and that's the bottom line.

Once our cats had switched to a more natural diet, we soon noticed a stark illustration of grain's filler effect: their litter-tray "output", as it were, had dramatically reduced.

DURING A CAT'S FIRST YEAR OF LIFE

For every 1 cup measure of raw meat cat food that goes in this end...

approximately 1 teaspoon of poop comes out this end.

THAT IS A BIO-AVAILABILITY EFFICIENCY RATE OF 95%

(And no, we didn't actually measure it with a teaspoon, but judging by what Penny habitually consumes and produces in her early life, it's not far off).

To get back to the story of our own cats' health problems, we felt that we were caught up in a vicious circle. We'd bought commercial cat food because we'd believed the advertising. The commercial cat food had made our cats sick, so we bought more cat food — medicated with a drug that tried to solve the problem the original cat food had caused, and which the grain-content of the medicated food continued to stimulate.

In Mehetabel's case, the medication kept ahead (more-or-less, and with regular vet visits) of the problem; in Jet's case, it didn't. So much so, that back in 2010 we felt certain we would lose her.

We wanted to break free. We wanted to spend as many years as we could with our beloved housemates — quality time, not miserably watching them decline from diseases caused by their food — and so we have. We have gathered that experience into the compendium of techniques and recipes presented in this book, because we feel they offer one of the best chances for the healthy longevity of the cats who enhance our lives.

Ground Meat-and-Bones or Prey-Based Diet?

This question provokes debate among proponents of raw-meat-based diets for cats. Before going further, let's define the meaning of the two terms:

- Ground Meat-and-Bones is the diet we describe in this book. Most of the ingredients are ground up, so that the cat doesn't have to deal with whole bones (or even significant bone fragments). It is however possible to add chunks of meat, or bonier parts, as part of this diet.

- Prey-based diets provide food that's closer to the cat's natural prey — for example, whole rodents, small poultry or game birds, or fish; or alternatively, parts of larger carcasses.

The idea behind the prey-based diet is that it's closer to what your cat would consume in the wild, and that emulating that experience as closely as possible will produce the happiest, healthiest animal. Proponents of prey-based diets make the point that in the natural world, a cat would be living off whatever birds and small mammals it could catch, and that providing ground food imposes an extra layer of artificiality on the cat.

While we considered a prey-based diet for our cats, and fully support those who choose to provide it, we ultimately chose a ground-food diet for the following reasons:

- Pragmatism: we are convinced that it would have been virtually impossible to persuade Jet and Mehetabel to accept a prey-based diet, particularly given the time pressure imposed by their urinary tract disease. Even when young, neither of them ever showed any interest in consuming prey that they caught; they don't recognise such things as food.

- Convenience: it's relatively easy to pre-prepare a large batch of ground food for freezing; the product is compact and can be stored in regular-shaped tubs that stack conveniently in the freezer.

- Freedom: we feel comfortable in asking friends or neighbors to defrost and feed ground food (it's really not that different from asking them to feed the contents of a tin can) so using this form of raw food doesn't affect our freedom to be away from home. By way of contrast, we wouldn't necessarily feel okay about asking someone to defrost and feed rodents or small birds.

- Economy: we like the fact that there's virtually zero waste with our ground food; the cats' bowls are routinely emptied. Also, the ground-food recipes are based on ingredients that are reasonably economical to buy.

- Safety: we are concerned that there is a risk of choking on bones or bone splinters when you allow a cat to crunch anything larger than a mouse or a sparrow.

- Supplementation: with ground food, it's very easy to add supplements or hydration (in other words, extra water) tailored to a cat's individual needs.

- Flexibility: there is no reason not to provide prey-style menu options as well, if your cat enjoys them.

The key is defining the correct balance for you and the cat you share a life with. Discovering the happy place to draw a line between *debilitating conveniences* and *life-enhancing conveniences* is crucial. To us, the kind of human/cat interaction that is balanced with wisdom, affection and respect so that the lives of all concerned can be enriched by close proximity, is the best kind of natural there is.

Cats with Pre-Existing Health Problems

If your cat has a pre-existing health problem, you would be wise to discuss the possibility of a raw food diet with your vet, before making the switch. We don't say this because we believe that staying on a grain-based commercial diet as opposed to a raw food diet can *ever* be better for your cat (we don't!), but rather because your vet will be able to advise you on how the raw food diet might interact with your cat's existing health problem, and recommend any tweaks, supplements or feeding regimens that could be helpful.

For example, the ability to administer extra water mixed into the ground food turned out to be particularly important to both cats who were suffering from urinary tract problems. Our vet made it very clear to us that *the single most important thing we could do to help these problems was to increase the cats' water intake.* In the past, that meant messing around with bulbs or syringes. Now, it's no more complicated than adding a little extra water to each dish of ground food and mixing it in.

MAKING THE SWITCH

TO

A

RAW FOOD

DIET

Making the Switch to a Raw Food Diet

We found that some of our cats accepted raw food quite readily, while others had to be persuaded. Penny, introduced to raw food as a kitten, was clearly delighted with it. With older cats, it's easier to make the transition over time, but it's also possible to persuade some reluctant cats to make the switch quickly — as we were forced to do with Jet, who we felt simply could not continue to eat commercial food given the effect it was having on her urinary health.

Important!

One thing you must *not* do is to try to starve your cat into making the switch, taking the attitude of, "She will eat if she is hungry." A cat needs regular meals, otherwise its liver will start processing fat into energy. If this continues for too long, fat can build up in the liver leading to liver failure due to Feline Hepatic Lipidosis (so-called "Fatty Liver Syndrome"). This disease is potentially lethal and will require veterinary intervention should it occur.

Susceptibility to Feline Hepatic Lipidosis varies from cat to cat — obesity is a risk factor — and anyone whose cat has undergone a major planned operation will probably have witnessed their pet not eating a day or so (counting from the evening before when pre-operation fasting starts, through to late in the following day when the cat is feeling well enough to be interested in food again). Still, we feel it's important to be aware of this issue when moving a cat to a new diet.

The Step-by-Step Method

This is the first method to try if you're not in a hurry. Take your time, don't make it stressful, don't push the cat; the transition is much easier to accomplish over a matter of weeks rather than days:

1. First, put a bit of raw meat food on your finger and let your cat smell it, then quickly swipe a little around their mouths and let them go. That's it; don't stress them about it.

2. Dip a few of your cat's dry food kibbles in the raw meat food before adding them back to the bowl, then let your cat carry on as usual.

3. Add a few small pieces of the raw meat food to your cat's dry food. They may pick around the new food at first but as they become accustomed they will snorfle it up along with the dry food without turning a hair.

4. Gradually shift the balance to favor increasing amounts of raw food to the point where it's mainly raw with one or two kibbles on top for decoration. At this point, you can start leaving the cereal off all together and, hey! Your cat has made the switch.

If your cat is presently on wet food as opposed to dry kibble, you'll obviously need to adapt the above steps accordingly. The principle remains the same.

The "Old Wives'" Method — Recommended by Jet

We've already mentioned that Jet was suffering badly from urinary tract problems when we decided to switch her to raw food, so much so that we didn't feel we had the leisure for a gradual transition — yet Jet showed no sign that she recognized anything other than her usual foil packet products as food.

However, we recalled a so-called Old Wives' Tale, as recounted by one of our mothers, which purports to be an infallible method of keeping a cat who has been taken to a new home from trying to return to the old one. The trick, apparently, is to put a dab of butter onto the cat's paws. The cat sits there and licks the butter off, and is so distracted (or delighted) by the pleasurable taste that she forgets about her previous home.

Or something.

Anyway, what's indisputable is that a typical cat doesn't like leaving foreign matter on its paws, and will try to clean itself of butter (or anything else) that is put there. So we smeared some of our ground raw food onto Jet's paws, and sure enough, she licked them clean. We repeated the process, and so did she. After a while she'd had enough and stopped bothering to clean herself — but the hurdle had been surmounted, she'd found that this unfamiliar product was actually quite tasty once she'd let herself try it, and thereafter she accepted it readily.

Prepping with Tasty Natural Treats

Cats like familiarity, in their diets as well as in other things. But they also like treats. Even when we were feeding commercial cat food, we occasionally offered treats such as small amounts of raw liver, pieces of lamb's hearts, ground beef, and so on. Essentially, raw meat that was in the process of being prepared for our own consumption.

Not all our cats were interested in these treats, but for those who were we feel it may have helped them to understand and remember that raw meat is food.

What's the Average Body Temperature of a Mouse?

(In case you're interested: it's about the same as the body temperature of a healthy human, apparently.)

When you are getting your cat accustomed to the change, avoiding serving it at fridge-temperature can help in some cases. If we give Jet cold food it often hits her stomach and promptly bounces right out again onto the floor. Like many cats, she does better with food that's closer to body temperature. Unfortunately, this can introduce a host of sanitary issues; after all, warm, raw meat is one of the world's best breeding grounds for bacteria.

So, if you warm your cat's food before serving it is imperative to set out an amount that you know your cat will be able to finish, and promptly clear away (and dispose of) any leftovers after 30 minutes. Of course, the safe period will depend on the ambient temperature in your home. We live in an old, cold cottage in an old, cold country so our other cats have become accustomed to chilly food. Even in summer our floors are cold, and in winter they are like an ice rink, which buys us a good couple of hours for them to finish up their portion.

Some people prefer to put the portion they are about to serve in a baggie and dip it like a tea bag in a bowl of hot water, but we never seem to able to get all the food out of the plastic bag after it has warmed. Instead, we place the food in a bowl, then place that bowl in a larger bowl in which we have added hot water and let it sit for three minutes. Then we lift the bowl out, stir and serve. The warmed bowl ensures that the food stays at body temperature for long enough to be consumed.

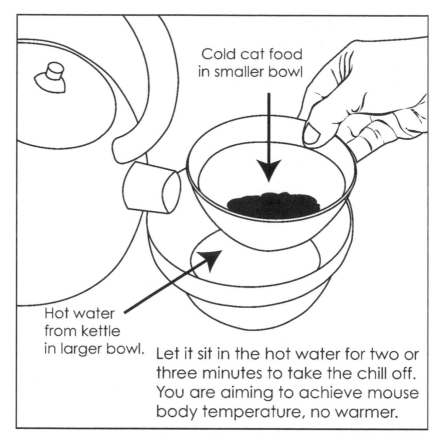

Cold cat food in smaller bowl

Hot water from kettle in larger bowl. Let it sit in the hot water for two or three minutes to take the chill off. You are aiming to achieve mouse body temperature, no warmer.

Happy Heating!

Important!

Don't use the microwave to heat your cat's raw food. The tiny bits of bone can become brittle when heated and are subsequently as dangerous as feeding your cat splinters of broken glass.

Possible Short-Term Effects of the Switch

Beside the major urinary health improvements that we were looking for, we noticed two further short-term effects. One was positive and one was negative, though only because of a pre-existing problem caused by years spent on a grain-based commercial diet.

Sweeter Breath

The positive effect was an improvement in our cats' dental health. Both Jet and Mehetabel had suffered from extremely bad breath that got better after each tooth-descaling session at the vet, but that gradually returned thereafter, even with regular brushing.

Once completely switched to raw food, we found that the cats' bad breath disappeared. We now believe that the starchy/sugary content of commercial grain-based food was as bad for our cats' dental health, as it was for their urinary health.

Lazy Bowels

A cat that is used to a grain-based diet can develop "lazy bowels", meaning that the cat's bowel function has come to rely on the extra roughage provided by the grain. Deprived of this, the cat can become constipated. Symptoms include going for days without defecating, distress when handled (particularly when applying pressure to the abdomen), loss of appetite and vitality, straining to go—or going—in inappropriate places, and even diarrhea. Extreme cases require veterinary intervention.

Following the switch, it became clear that Mehetabel suffered from lazy bowels. As a short-term cure, our vet recommended oral dosing with food-grade mineral oil; 3ml administered daily with a syringe over a few days did the trick. Vaseline® (100% pure petroleum jelly, as contained in some commercial hairball remedies) has a similar function. To avoid interference with digestion, it's best not to administer either of these remedies at meal times, or for extended periods.

The vet's longer-term recommendation was to increase the cats' water intake, something that was also helpful for their urinary systems and that we accomplished by adding more water to the ground food.

A third option would have been to incorporate roughage such as psyllium husk into the cats' food, however our vet advised that this would not necessarily help — apparently it can make the problem worse with some cats. Also, we felt that it was excess bulk that had caused the lazy bowels in the first place, so that moving back in that direction would have been more of a palliative than a cure. On the other hand, the option is there for you to explore if you find that extra water isn't enough to keep your cat's bowels working smoothly.

TOOLS & TECHNIQUES TO ENHANCE YOUR CAT'S LONGEVITY and GOOD HEALTH

Tools and Techniques

Grinder/Mincer

Would you like to hear about the biggest financial mistake we made when we were starting out with raw cat food? It was investing in a popular, big-name-brand electric meat grinder/mincer. We chose a powerful model with mostly good online reviews — sadly for us, it turned out that we should have taken more note of the few negative ones, which spoke of poor performance and ridiculous noise levels.

There was no reason in this sparkly universe that a machine needs to be geared as high as this one was to turn an auger at a slow rate; it was deafening and reminiscent of the world's largest dental convention testing all their drills simultaneously.

Constant blockages made it very slow work, meaning that we had to wear ear protection for the entire two hours it took to process three chickens. When the job was finally done, the resulting product was warm to the touch; the machine wasn't cleanly grinding or mincing the chickens, as much as laboriously squishing them into a warm paste. We couldn't bear the noise and inefficiency of this electric grinder, so we decided to chalk it up as a loss and move on.

The replacement we chose was a hand-cranked Porkert (No. 12) grinder/mincer. Manufactured from tinned cast-iron in the Czech Republic, the Porkert is smooth as silk and almost effortless to turn when processing meat (it does require some work when grinding small bones, but not nearly as much as you probably expect if you've never tried it). It's pleasantly quiet, hassle-free, and much faster than the electric monster; we reckon it grinds the same amount of meat in one quarter of the time.

Porkert is not the only manufacturer of hand-cranked grinders or mincers, of course. Particularly if you live in the USA, you will find a wide variety to choose from. We offer the following suggestions to help you make that choice:

- A heavier-duty machine will handle small bones more easily. Consider getting a model that bolts to your kitchen table or worktop, rather than one of the lighter-duty models that fastens with a clamp.

- The cutting blades inside a grinder/mincer are durable and can be re-sharpened once they become blunt (see below) but after long use you may need to replace them, so it makes sense to choose a model for which spares are reliably available.

- If you also plan to use your grinder/mincer as part of your regular kitchen routine, then pay attention to the other fittings or accessories that you might need — specialist nozzles, or coarser/finer cutting discs, for example — and ensure they are available to fit the model you choose.

Assembly, Disassembly and Sharpening

At the heart of your hand-operated meat grinder is an auger that presses chunks of meat against a perforated steel plate, while also turning a set of cutting blades against that plate. The cutting blades slice through the meat, while the action of the auger forces the resulting fragments through the holes in the perforated plate. The fineness of the grind depends on the diameter of the holes.

A threaded ring presses the plate against the cutting blades. The ring needs to be tightened to position the plate flush against the blades, with the two components fitting snugly together, otherwise you will not achieve a satisfactory grind (you will keep turning the handle but little or nothing will be produced).

With a new grinder that hasn't yet been worn in, the fit of the plate into the machine may be overly tight; in such cases a hammer can help both in fitting the plate and tightening/releasing the ring; see the illustrations opposite. Similarly, if you find it difficult to remove the perforated plate from the machine, a few gentle taps from the handle end of the auger will quickly loosen it (remove the handle first). *When using a hammer to tighten or loosen parts, be gentle!* Aim to use multiple light taps instead of a few heavy ones; you don't want to damage the machine.

After a few sessions you will notice that turning the grinder gets to be harder work. This is a sign that the blades need sharpening with wet-and-dry abrasive paper as shown on the two-page spread overleaf. Lay the paper on a true flat surface such as a tempered glass worktop protector, sprinkle liberally with water, and proceed as shown.

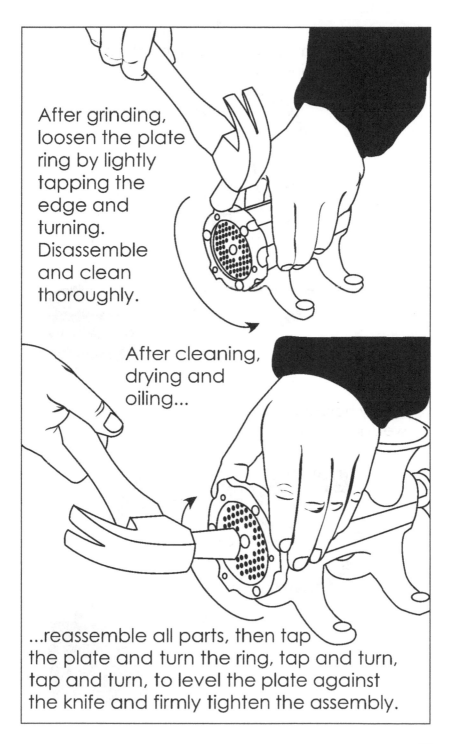

After grinding, loosen the plate ring by lightly tapping the edge and turning. Disassemble and clean thoroughly.

After cleaning, drying and oiling...

...reassemble all parts, then tap the plate and turn the ring, tap and turn, tap and turn, to level the plate against the knife and firmly tighten the assembly.

1. Fifty vertical figure eights on medium grit wet/dry sanding paper

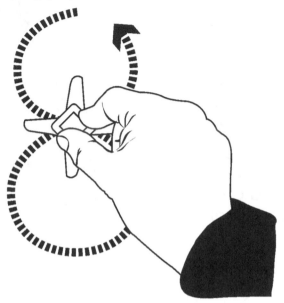

2. Fifty horizontal figure eights on medium grit wet/dry sanding paper

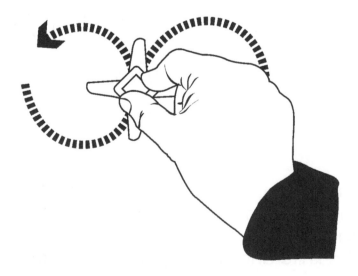

3. Now, spin the blade 1/8 turn and do fifty vertical figure eights on medium grit wet/dry sanding paper

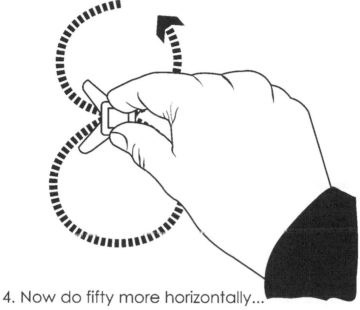

4. Now do fifty more horizontally...

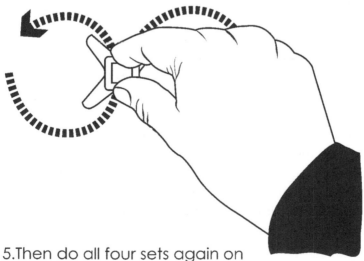

5.Then do all four sets again on fine-grit wet/dry paper... Sharp!

The Heavy Butcher's Cleaver

Our second essential tool is a heavy butcher's cleaver, one that's capable of chopping through meat and small bones in one easy movement. Ours is 16 inches (42cm) long overall with a 10-inch (26cm) blade, and weighs 2lb 12oz or 1.25kg. This is over three times as heavy as our domestic Chinese cleaver, which is frankly not really up to the job of preparing whole chickens for the grinder. We would use the Chinese cleaver in a pinch, but it would be harder work and there would always be the risk of denting the blade.

Something like a chef's knife, or the kind of toy cleaver that often comes in a presentation box with a set of kitchen knives, would simply not be appropriate for the task — not least because they may be made of relatively brittle alloys, with the corresponding risk of leaving sharp fragments of metal behind when they encounter bone.

We found our heavy cleaver in an antique centre, and suspect it was there due to health-and-safety regulations that require professional butchers to get rid of "unsanitary" wooden (or wooden-handled) implements and cutting boards. At the time of writing, eBay still allows "vintage" cleavers to be sold, and they often seem to be exactly the sort of retired butcher's cleaver that we prefer for this job.

Other possible sources include garage sales, flea markets or junk shops. A few heavy-duty cleavers are also offered by regular online retailers, but do look at the size and weight specifications and read the reviews before you buy. Alternatively, if you're lucky enough to live near a traditional butcher's shop, it can't do any harm to ask if they can point you in the right direction!

We believe that the best old cleavers are carbon steel and though they do not look factory bright they will keep a good edge and serve you well for the rest of your life. All they ask of you is an occasional good whetstone sharpening followed up by a few swipes on a steel after each use. Carbon blades are superior in every way to modern stainless steel and though they may take some effort to find, it's like discovering treasure when you do.

The Mighty Cleaver.

Consider the possibilities. Accept no substitutes.

Other Tools

You'll also need:

- a set of kitchen weighing scales, plus measuring spoons if needed for small amounts
- a sharp boning knife or other small, thin-bladed kitchen knife
- a stout pair of kitchen scissors or poultry shears
- a large spoon
- a large, sturdy chopping board
- a receiving tray or plate under the grinder
- two large mixing bowls, so that you can process meat from one into the other. Dishwashing tubs are better than regular mixing bowls if you plan to make bulk quantities
- a needle or thumbtack for piercing soft gel capsules
- freezer-safe plastic containers with snap-tight lids — sufficient to store the batch you intend to make.

For clean-up, hygiene and maintenance:

- wet-and-dry abrasive paper in 600 grit and 120 grit
- nylon brushes/bottle-brushes
- a light hammer, if needed to loosen overly-tight grinder parts
- mineral oil, to protect steel grinder parts from rust
- household bleach for before-and-after sanitizing
- latex gloves, if you dislike the feel of raw meat on your hands
- an apron.

Cleaning Up

At the end of the process, the various tools and grinder parts will be covered with meat and bone fragments and must be carefully cleaned, taking care not to contaminate any regular dishwashing equipment (sponges, brushes etc.) that will be required again, since meat and bone fragments can be difficult to remove. Much of the debris can simply be rinsed away under a gently running tap.

Take care to remove all the cartilage, bone and meat fragments from inside the grinder. Don't try to feed this debris to your cat, since it may contain bone splinters that will cause injury if ingested. Chalk it up to the cost of doing business and discard it.

A large round-headed nylon brush, reserved for that purpose, is a convenient tool for giving the inside of the grinder a final, thorough scrubbing. Similarly, wash the grinder parts with hot water and detergent. Use a bamboo skewer or similar tool to clear out any fragments lodged in the grinding plate holes, then thoroughly wash the grinder parts in hot water and detergent and air-dry completely. Before reassembly, wipe the screw threads with some mineral oil to prevent rust.

After the washing up is done, fill a bucket with water, add a small splash of bleach, and wipe down anything that may have been touched or splashed with specks of meat — for example, tables, kitchen furniture, and if you've been particularly messy, the floor and perhaps the soles of your shoes!

THE RECIPE

The Recipes

We offer our cats two recipes, one based on chicken and one based on beef or lamb. The second recipe is *either* beef *or* lamb; you shouldn't mix the meat/offal of different species in a single batch of food.

The Main Recipe

This is the chicken recipe that we feed most of the time. We offer the supplementary beef/lamb recipe (described in the following pages) a couple of times a week, to give our cats the opportunity to eat kidney and heart. This kidney and heart is not present in the chicken recipe, though there would be no harm in adding modest amounts, similar to the amount of liver, of these to the chicken mix if you can get the appropriate chicken offal. That said, a couple of our cats have chosen to eat the following chicken recipe almost exclusively, and have done so in good health for two years.

Ingredients

Whole Chickens (*bones, skin and meat*)	6kg or 13lb 4oz
Chicken Livers	300g or 10oz
Taurine	12g or 2 tsp
Iodized salt	12g or 1 tsp
Raw Egg Yolks (*remove all egg white*)	12
Salmon or other fish oil	12 x 1000mg capsules
Vitamin E	12 x 400IU capsules
Water	500ml or 2 cups

Preparing the Chicken

1. Use a sharp knife to remove the chicken legs and wings. Separate the thighs from the drumsticks, then remove the thick leg bones from these portions. Either discard these bones, or set them aside for the stock-pot if you wish to use them in your own cooking.

2. If desired, or to promote dental health by providing chewing exercise, cut off the wing tips and some slices of muscle to feed separately.

3. Remove and discard any loose cartilage from the thigh or wing joints that you've just exposed; these pieces of cartilage won't go through the grinder/mincer but they *will* tend to clog it.

4. Use the butcher's cleaver, poultry shears or stout kitchen scissors to chop up the rest of the carcass into manageable chunks.

5. Again using the cleaver, reduce bony parts such as the wings, ribs and backbone into smaller fragments. The better you reduce these small bones, the easier the grinding process will be. Don't let fly as if you were chopping wood; it's best to keep the front corner of the cleaver's blade pressed against the chopping board (use your secondary hand to steady the blade), while pivoting the handle to the left and right as well as up and down, so that you can cover an entire piece of chicken with the arc formed by the pivoting cleaver. See the illustration opposite. The effect is of repeated crushing, as much as chopping. If fragments of chicken or bone are flying across the work area, you're being too vigorous.

Grinding the Chicken and Liver

Grind the meat, crushed bone and offal on a medium disc, then again on a fine disc. We've found our cats are fine with the medium grind alone, but yours may differ so play it safe at first. Hand grinding is moderately hard work, but if you're just not making progress then the grinder is probably clogged up; open it and clear it. If you find lots of rubbery cartilage inside the mechanism, you need to take more care to remove it from the carcasses. And if you're really having problems with grinding, you either need to revisit the bone-crushing stage, or to sharpen the grinder blade as described in the previous chapter.

the up and down movements on the handle end of the blade copies the crushing motion of a carnivore's teeth chewing and grinding meat and bone.

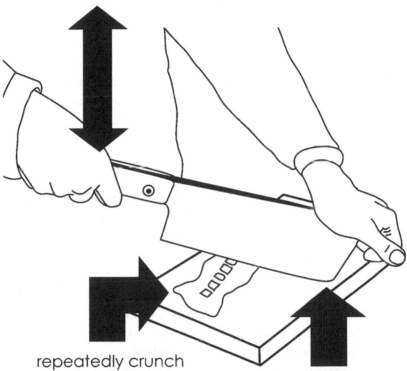

repeatedly crunch and break the wing, chest and back bones to expose the marrow on each chop in order to facilitate the passage of the meat and bone through the grinder blade.

the point of the cleaver maintains constant contact with the cutting board as you repeatedly chop and swivel the blade. **Never hammer the bone** with the blade, just pump the handle and pivot the point.

Mixing the Food

Measure and place in the large mixing bowl the egg yolks, salt, taurine, salmon/fish oil, vitamin E (pierce and squeeze the gels) and water as well as any special supplements like glucosamine sulfate, psyllium and so on according to your cat's individual requirements (see next chapter). Roll up your sleeves, thoroughly wash your hands, tip the ground meat and bones into the bowl containing the rest of the ingredients and mix it all together carefully and well. If you have an open cut on your skin, wear latex or dishwashing gloves while doing this.

Spoon the appropriate amount in individual plastic snap-lid bowls, taking care to leave at least a half inch gap between the top of the food and the lid to allow room for freezing expansion. Place however much you need for immediate use in the fridge, and freeze the rest.

The Supplementary Recipe

This recipe is based on either lamb or beef, and provides a wider range of offal than the chicken recipe (simply because chicken offal is not nearly as easy to find in our local shops as lamb and beef offal). We offer this recipe a couple of times a week.

Since lamb and sheep bones can't be processed through a domestic grinder, and since cats are not inclined to stalk and bring down such large animals, this recipe does not include bones, but rather the food-grade bone meal that's sold as a nutritional supplement — don't use the stuff intended for fertilizing the garden!

Grind the offal, or simply chop it into manageable chunks if your cat enjoys larger pieces. Place the meat and offal in a large mixing bowl, add the other ingredients, mix until all the ingredients are thoroughly blended and freeze in small portions.

Important!

Excessive vitamin A can cause liver damage in cats and can potentially kill them. Since liver is rich in vitamin A, don't be tempted to increase the liver content of either recipe, even if your cat enjoys the taste. Take similar care if supplementing with fish-liver oils such as cod-liver oil.

Ingredients

Lamb or beef (Ground/Minced)	2kg or 4lb 8oz
Matching Liver (Lamb or beef as appropriate)	100g or 4oz
Matching Heart	100g or 4oz
Matching Kidney	100g or 4oz
Taurine	4g or 2/3 tsp
Iodized salt	4g or 1/3 tsp
Bone Meal (Food Grade Supplement)	4 tablespoons
Raw Egg Yolks (remove all egg white)	4
Salmon or other fish oil	4 x 1000mg capsules
Vitamin E	4 x 400IU capsules
Water	250ml or 1 cup

TREATS & SUPPLEMENTS

Treats and Supplements

Treats

Raw meat from animals such as pheasant, duck, venison, beef and lamb can be served as occasional treats, though please don't try to make a batch of cat food from beef mixed with chicken liver; you should not mix innards from one animal with the flesh of another.

Tinned pilchards, sardines and tuna should only be considered occasional treats as well, since they lack vital nutrients. Raw fish is a no-no. Uncooked fish bones can be deadly when swallowed — and not a painless death, either.

Supplements

Many cats have individual dietary requirements that will need to be addressed by you now (in consultation with your vet, if necessary), rather than by supplemented commercial food. A basic common sense approach should be fine in most cases. Supplement amounts given below correspond to the full chicken recipe; when making larger or smaller amounts, adjust accordingly:

- If your cats are thin, feed them all the chicken skin. If they are overweight, leave some of it out.

- If your cats are elderly or suffering joint pain, add twelve 500mg capsules of glucosamine sulfate powder to the main recipe; simply separate the capsules, sprinkle the powder and mix in to all the other ingredients before packaging and freezing.

- You can boost your cat's fluid intake by adding water. Your cat may reject the mixture if it's too soupy, so proceed with care.

- Any stomach upset can be safely eased by the addition of probiotics — twelve powdered Lactobacillus capsules added to the batch should do the trick, or you can try two teaspoons of living bio-yogurt mixed into an individual serving.

- You may also substitute a tin of mackerel, salmon or sardines for the fish oil.

- Cats rarely need roughage, but if you are convinced they do, mix a tablespoon of psyllium husk into the batch.

This small book in your hand is the culmination of extensive study, trial and development in the quest to benefit the lives of the cats we love and, in turn, to increase our enjoyment of the time we are priveleged to share with them.

But it's far from the last word on the subject; now it's your turn to take up the torch. Read, ask questions, refine what we have written in these pages with your own discoveries and share what you learn with others.

A contented cat who chooses you to share a life with is a pleasure to be around, and a healthy, happy, active, affectionate cat is a gift. The only question that remains is, *How much effort is that gift worth to you?*

> *"The smallest feline is a masterpiece"*
> — *Leonardo da Vinci*

CPSIA information can be obtained at www.ICGtesting.com
Printed in the USA
BVOW08s0933040614

355387BV00010B/481/P